Garnishing

Easy, artful food decoration

Making the ordinary extraordinary!

Garnishing

Easy, artful food decoration

Making the ordinary extraordinary!

Rudolf Biller

Mud Puddle Books
NEW YORK

Garnishing:
Easy, artful food decoration
Making the ordinary extraordinary!

Originally published as:
Garnieren und Verzieren. Köstlich zubereiten—liebevoll anrichten
by Rudolf Biller
© 1986 by Falken Verlag, a division of Verlagsgruppe Random House GmbH,
München, Germany

Translation © 2005 , 2010 by
Mud Puddle Books, Inc.

Published by
Mud Puddle Books, Inc.
54 W. 21st Street
Suite 601
New York, NY 10010

info@mudpuddlebooks.com

ISBN: 978-1-60311-072-3

English translation by Katja Yeats

Printed and bound in China

Contents

Introduction

Eating with Your Eyes

Who can doubt that food that appeals to the eye will taste better and increase our joy? That's the basis of garnishing, to make the ordinary extraordinary. What's best is that you don't have to be a professional to achieve professional results—and you'll have a great time doing it.

This book is an easy-to-follow, heavily illustrated step-by-step introduction to the world of garnishing that will allow you to unleash your creativity and produce art that's edible. Garnishing is highly festive and is as perfect a complement for daily meals as for special occasions. Every meal becomes memorable when you add that little extra something. Not only will you and your family be pleased, your friends will be delighted and impressed.

Meals are planned to achieve a happy balance of color and flavor and garnishing provides an exciting visual enhancement. Great garnishing secrets are at hand! No longer will you just serve food, you'll make a presentation—and you'll be the talk of the table.

CITRUS FRUIT

LEMON AND LIME

Lemons and limes are available year round at most grocery stores as well as fine produce sections in specialty stores and delicatessens.

Today lemons, which originated in India, come largely from southern California as well as Italy (Sicily) and Spain. Limes also originated in Southeast Asia. Flourishing in tropical climates, limes today are likely to come from Florida, Mexico, Italy, Spain and India. Lemons and limes are closely related even though the color of their peel and their size are different. Limes have a thin, bright green peel and are smaller than lemons.

ORANGE

The orange is another citrus fruit developed in Southeast Asia. Although there are more than 400 varieties known, the orange is generally divided into two types. Blonde oranges such as Valencia, Navel and Jaffa are pale-skinned juicy oranges available year round. Blood oranges have a red-tinged flesh known for its

7

sweetness and are available from December to mid-March. The leading orange-producing country in the world is Brazil followed by the United States (Florida and California), Mexico, Spain, Italy, China, Egypt, Turkey, Morocco and Greece.

MANDARIN

Mandarins are smaller than oranges with a peel that loosely surrounds the fruit and is easily removed. Mandarins, native to Southeast Asia and the Philippines, include all varieties of tangerines. When buying fresh mandarins, seedless types such as the Clementine are preferable.

Mandarins are also available in cans. Canned mandarins have already been peeled and are therefore particularly well suited for garnishing.

WHAT SHOULD YOU KEEP IN MIND WHEN BUYING CITRUS FRUIT?

Degree of ripeness: Fruits should have a fresh, plump peel and resist pressure when touched. A wrinkled peel is not only unsightly for garnishing purposes, but it also indicates that the fruit is old. Fruits with the least bit of mold should never be used!

Note: A deep green peel on a lime indicates that the fruit is ripe.

TREATED FRUITS

After they are harvested, most citrus fruit—with the exception of limes—are specially treated in order to preserve and protect them against blue and green molds. To do so, the peel is coated with wax and treated with preservatives. Even washing citrus fruit with hot water will not remove the preservatives. If you want to use the peel we recommend you use untreated citrus fruit. However, you should also wash untreated citrus fruit before using.

TOOLS

Smooth cuts of lemons and limes are made with a small kitchen knife. The larger diameters of oranges require a medium to large knife.

A channel knife is used to cut grooves in the orange and lemon peel. If the fruit is sliced after grooves have been cut the slices will look like cartwheels. Eight to ten different sized cutters are used to cut out slices of lemon, lime or orange. If a cutter has a smooth edge it is easy to separate the peel from the flesh by simply turning the cutter.

CITRUS FRUIT

SLICES
Slices of lemons, oranges and limes make delightful garnishes.

CUTTING GROOVES
Grooves are cut into the peel of a whole fruit using a channel knife. After cutting the grooves, slice the fruit. Thick slices are used to place on the edge of a glass or for a simple garnish of fruit slices spread out on a platter. Thin slices are ideal for twisting.

CUT UP SLICES
Smooth or grooved slices can be cut in halves, quarters or eighths.

CUTTING OUT
Using a smooth or grooved round cutter, cut out the flesh of $3/16$ to $5/16$" (5 to 7 mm) thick slices of citrus fruit. Make sure that no peel is left on the cut out slice.

CITRUS FAN
Arrange 3 to 4 half slices in the shape of a fan.

Orange slice cut into sixths with Maraschino cherry and truffle or black garnishing paste

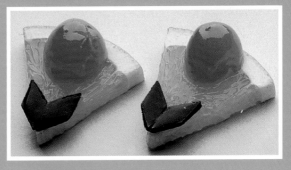

Grooved lemon slices with cherry tomatoes, diamond shaped scallion slice and a dot of truffle

Cut out slice of orange with melon ball and truffle tips

Lemon slices cut in half with smooth or grooved peel, garnished with slices of stuffed olives, diamond shaped scallion slice or melon balls

Orange slices with cut out, half moon shaped red peppers and melon ball

Grooved slice of lemon with hearts of red peppers

Cut out slice of orange with tomato-scallion flower and truffle ellipses

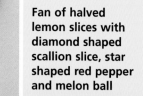

Fan of halved lemon slices with diamond shaped scallion slice, star shaped red pepper and melon ball

12

Make a slice or a half
of a lemon with bow

CITRUS FRUIT

NOTCHED SLICES

Make a cut to the middle of a smooth or grooved slice of citrus fruit. To form a funnel, use a thin, notched slice and push the two ends on top of each other. To form a spiral, use a thin slice and twist one cut side to the front, the other to the back. To form a line of spirals, twist several spirals and stagger them behind one another.

WEDGES

Cut a citrus fruit in half lengthwise and cut each half into four to five wedges.

ORANGE FILETS

On either end of an orange or lemon, cut off the peel down to the flesh. Cut the remaining peel as close to the flesh as possible. Then, using a sharp knife, cut out the individual filets.

SLICES OR HALVES WITH A BOW

Using a slice of citrus fruit cut the peel from the flesh almost all the way around. Fold the strip of peel into a knot. Using a halved citrus fruit, cut a 3/16" (5 mm) strip of peel at a slight angle almost all the way around and fold it into a knot.

Fan of three lemon spirals on top of a grooved lemon slice with olive

Lemon funnel with three Maraschino cherries and diamond shaped scallion slices

GARNISH FOR GLASSES
Cut a lemon into quarters or eighths. Cut about 1³⁄₁₆" (3 cm) of peel from the flesh, but do not cut the peel off. Hang the lemon wedge by the cut peel on the rim of a glass.

14

SEEDED AND PITTED FRUIT

APPLE

Apples have been part of mankind's history and mythology for more than 8,000 years. Worldwide, there are more than 20,000 cultivated varieties of apples in an endless array of sizes, textures and tastes. However, apple trees grow best in moderate climate zones where they produce perfectly balanced apples: refreshingly tart and deliciously sweet.

Because of their diversity, apples are available year round. Among the most popular varieties are Red Delicious, Golden Delicious, McIntosh, Rome, Winesap, Gala and Fuji.

APPLES FOR GARNISHES AND DECORATIONS

Before using them for garnishes, apples should be specially treated since their flesh quickly turns brown after peeling or cutting. To avoid discoloration, cut apples should either be poached (see page 18), brushed with lemon juice wherever they have been cut or coated with aspic.

PEAR

More than 5,000 varieties of pears have been cultivated. We differentiate between table pears whose flesh is juicy, white, and sweet and cooking pears that are fairly firm and not very juicy. Because the pear harvest is relatively short and the fruit spoils quickly, canned pears are frequently used for cooking. Popular pear varieties include Bartlett, Bosc and D'Anjou.

PEACH

There are more than 2,000 varieties of peaches. These fruits have velvety skin, firm, juicy flesh and a large pit. Peaches are differentiated by varieties whose flesh comes off the pit easily (freestone) and those whose flesh sticks to the pit (clingstone). In the United States,

peaches are grown in 30 states with California producing the most. They are available beginning in April and peaking in late summer. From November to April peaches are imported from Mexico, Chile and New Zealand. Raspberries and strawberries are a good complement to peaches.

TOOLS

Using a vegetable peeler ensures that the pit fruit is peeled very thinly. The knife used to slice and cut pieces of pitted fruit must be rust free to prevent the fruit from discoloring. Apples are cut into even wedges using an apple wedger. Using the apple wedger also removes the core of the apple. Cutters are used to prepare apples for stuffing. A cutter with a 1⅜ to 1⅝" (3.5 to 4 cm) diameter is used to cut the inside. The cutter for the outer rim must be larger, about 2 to 2⅜" (5 to 6 cm) diameter and may have a grooved edge. Melon ballers of different sizes are used to remove the core and hollow the inside of an apple or pear for stuffing.

PEELING APPLES

Peel an apple in a spiral manner using a vegetable peeler. Use a melon baller to remove the core from apples that have been cut in halves. If a recipe calls for apple sections, cut out the core in a half moon shape using a small knife.

POACHING APPLES

Finish all of the cuts required for the garnish and poach the apple in white wine. Some sugar, lemon and a stick of cinnamon may be added to round off the flavor. Depending on how long the apple pieces are poached, their consistency is either soft or still crisp.

BREADING APPLES

After poaching, let the excess wine drip off the apple pieces and coat them with flour. Evenly brown the apples in a frying pan using butter.

Or: Coat the slices with flour, a lightly beaten egg and slivered almonds or coconut flakes. Fry the apple in clarified butter in a deep fryer or frying pan until golden brown.

Peeling

Coring

Poached apple slice

Slice coated with coconut flakes

Poached apple slice

Slice coated with almonds

Cut apple for stuffing

STEAMED APPLE FOR STUFFING

For this recipe, use a small variety of apple such as Pomme Gris or Cox's Orange Pippin. As a substitute, you may use larger apples that have been cut to size. Use different sized cutters (with either a smooth or grooved edge): a larger cutter for the outer rim, a smaller one for the inside, and a melon baller to remove the apple's core. Cut the outside of the apple with the larger cutter. Insert the smaller cutter about about ⅓" (1 cm) into the apple and remove the core using a melon baller. Make sure you do not damage the outer rim. Poach the prepared apples in a mixture of white wine, sugar, lemon peel, a clove and a cinnamon stick.

Apple with almond covered rim, stuffed with cranberries and melon ball

Poached apple slice with a slice of kiwi and a prune

Poached apple slice with sweet chestnut mousse, slivered almonds, and a strawberry

Apple stuffed with Maraschino cherries and diamond shaped scallion slices

Apple with pistachio covered rim, stuffed with sweet chestnut mousse and topped with a chestnut

Poached apple slice with pistachio covered rim, melon balls and Maraschino cherry

Apple segments with halved slices of kiwi, a prune, and pieces of strawberry

EXOTIC FRUIT

PINEAPPLE

Naturally sweet and juicy, fresh pineapple is available year round. This exotic Western Hemisphere native has many uses for garnishing. The degree of ripeness of a pineapple is determined by the color of the peel. The fruit is ripe if the color ranges from light orange to dark orange to copper red.

CORRECT STORAGE

Pineapple is delicate and it does not do well with pressure and cold. A good storage temperature is 64°F (18°C). Tie a piece of string around the pineapple just below the crown and hang it up to avoid too much pressure on the fruit.

BANANA

The banana is a sweet, tropical fruit that is usually eaten raw. However, bananas may also be cooked, fried and flambéed. For cooking purposes, it is best to use barely ripe bananas. For eating, it is best to use fully ripe bananas whose peel has little black spots. Bananas are best stored at room temperature. They should

not be packed too tightly in a
fruit bowl. Storing bananas in
the refrigerator interrupts the
ripening process and can give
them a bitter taste. Whenever
they are used as a garnish,
peeled bananas and cut surfaces
of the fruit should be sprinkled
with lemon juice to avoid
browning.

KIWI

Kiwis are about the size of an
egg with a brownish-green,
hairy peel that should not be
eaten. The flesh of a kiwi is
bright green, somewhat lighter
in the center, and has a ring of
small black seeds. The taste is refreshingly sour and aromatic and
somewhat resembles gooseber-
ries and melon. Kiwis are well
suited for garnishing and deco-

23

rating because of their fresh green color and decorative appearance. Furthermore, they can be stored for quite a while. Fresh kiwis are available year round. Ripe kiwis give slightly when touched. If stored in the vegetable bin of the refrigerator, they may last for two to three weeks.

MELON

There are several different varieties of melons—here is a small selection:

Honeydew melon: oval shape, lemon-yellow rind with very sweet flesh.

Cantaloupe melon: very sweet with bright orange flesh.

Persian melon: a large melon with a very sweet orange flesh

Watermelon: sweet and juicy, summer's most popular treat

WHAT SHOULD YOU KEEP IN MIND WHEN BUYING MELONS?

The degree of ripeness of a melon is not determined by the color of the rind but rather by smell and pressure. Ripe melons smell like pineapple and musk. At the same time, they should give when pressure is applied around the blossom area. Melons should be stored in the vegetable bin of the refrigerator. They will last longer and taste better when thoroughly chilled.

TOOLS

Medium sized knifes are used to peel and cut melons. Remove the core of a pineapple with a cutter. A grapefruit knife is used to cut the flesh from the skin of a quartered pineapple. The flesh of melons is cut out with a melon baller. A corrugated knife is used to decoratively cut pieces of melon.

PEELING PINEAPPLE

Cut off the crown of a thoroughly washed pineapple. Starting from the crown end, cut about ⅝" (1.5 cm) thick strips toward the bottom. Cut out the eyes of the pineapple by lining up the knife's blade with the rows of eyes and cutting furrows in a diagonal pattern around the fruit.

PORTIONING PINEAPPLE

Vertically cut the pineapple into quarters or sixths. Remove the core by cutting down the length of each quarter or sixth. Cut off the skin and cut each section into six to eight pieces.

PORTIONED SLICES

Wash a pineapple and cut it into ⅝ to ¾" (1.5 to 2 cm) thick slices beginning from the bottom end. To cut out the core, use a circular cutter with a smooth edge and a diameter of about ¾ to 1" (2 to 2.5 cm). To cut the outside, use a cutter that leaves about ⅝" (1.5 cm) of rind. Cutting the skin this thick ensures that the eyes are removed.

GARNISHED SLICES

Decorate the middle or rim of a slice of pineapple with berries, cherries, asparagus tips or mousse.

Peeling

Removing eyes

Cutting portions

Coring

Cutting out

Slice and pieces of pineapple

25

PINEAPPLE BOAT

Lengthwise, cut a pineapple into eight wedges of equal size. Cut off a thin slice on the bottom of the wedges to ensure that they stand securely. Cut off about ¾" (2 cm) on the pointed side of the boat to remove the core of the pineapple. Using a sharp knife, cut bite size pieces down to about ¾" (2 cm) above the skin and stagger them on top of the skin. Garnish with Maraschino cherries and melon balls.

Pineapple boat

Halved slices of pineapple

HALVED SLICES

Put the round sides of two halved pineapple slices next to each other. Arrange two halved pineapple slices in the shape of an "S".

Fig-hedgehog on top of pineapple quarters

QUARTERED SLICES

Cut a slice of pineapple into quarters and arrange the pieces behind one another. Quarters can be segmented into even smaller pieces.

26

ROUND BANANA SLICES

Peel a banana and cut it into equal size slices. Arrange the slices behind one another or in the shape of a four-leaf clover.

OVAL BANANA SLICES

Cut a peeled banana into slices holding the knife at an angle. Oval slices are larger than round ones and can be arranged in the shape of a fan.

KIWI SLICES

Kiwis may be sliced lengthwise or crosswise. Peel the kiwi and cut it into equal size slices. Arrange the slices behind one another, overlapping them slightly. Slices may also be arranged in a circle. Decorate the middle of the circle with a tomato rose (see page 45).

KIWI CROWN

Using a pointed knife, pierce a kiwi all the way to the center and all the way around in a zigzag pattern. Carefully separate the two halves and slightly flatten the bottom by cutting off a thin slice.

Round and oval slices

Banana boat

Kiwi slices

Kiwi crown

Note: You can use either peeled or unpeeled kiwis for garnishes. Unpeeled kiwis are eaten with a spoon. So, if you use them in your decorations, be sure to provide dessert-spoons.

Oval banana slices with strawberry

27

BANANA BOAT

Using a sharp, pointed knife, score the banana about ⅛" (about 3 mm) deep and peel the skin backwards. Set the peel in place with a skewer and top it with a strawberry and prune. To stuff the banana, slice another banana and combine the slices with dark fruits.

Note: Banana garnishes should not be fixed until just before serving because the flesh of a banana discolors quickly. Even sprinkling a banana with lemon juice only helps for a short period of time.

Kiwi half with cranberry mousse, mandarin and walnut

Banana boat with fruit salad

Kiwi crown on mango slice with cranberry mousse, almond, and Maraschino cherry

Banana slices and kiwi crown with cranberry mousse and grape halves

Banana flower with Maraschino cherry

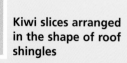

Kiwi slices arranged in the shape of roof shingles

PIECES OF MELON

Vertically cut the melon into six or eight wedges. Scrape out the seeds with a tablespoon and cut the flesh from the rind using a grapefruit knife. Cut the flesh into bite size pieces using a corrugated knife. When cutting, hold the knife either straight or at an angle.

STUFFED MELON WITH LID

Cut off the upper third of a washed melon. Scrape out the seeds with a tablespoon. Flatten the bottom side of the melon, so that it stands better. Stuff the carved melon with your favorite filling. Some filling suggestions are: strawberries in frothy port, orange filets with slivered almonds, pineapple with blackberries or any other kind of fruit salad. Using a decorative skewer, fasten the lid to the melon after it has been filled.

STUFFED MELON WITH RIM OF MELON BALLS

Cut the melon in half and scrape out the seeds using a tablespoon. Flatten the bottom sides of each melon half, so that it stands better. Using a melon baller, cut out eight balls from the inside of the melon and arrange them evenly spaced on the rim of the melon. Fill the melon with a fruit salad of your choice.

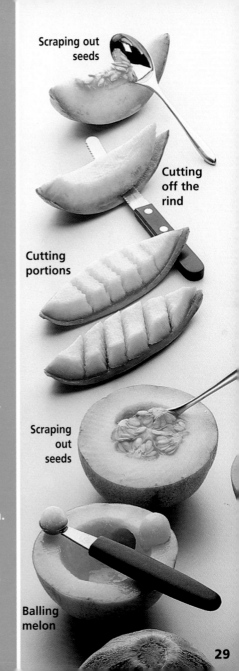

Scraping out seeds

Cutting off the rind

Cutting portions

Scraping out seeds

Balling melon

29

Melon
crown

Melon with black currant jello

MELON CROWN

Using a pointed knife, pierce a melon all the way around in a zigzag pattern. Separate the two halves by slightly turning them. Scrape out the seeds with a tablespoon.

MELON WITH JELLO

Cut a small melon in half and scrape out the seeds using a tablespoon. Set the melon half on top of a glass and fill it with black currant jello. Let the jello set in the refrigerator and cut into slices for garnishing.

Melon with rim of melon balls, filled with exotic fruit salad

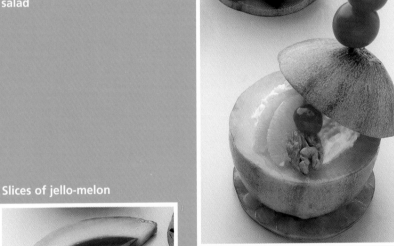

Slices of jello-melon

Top: melon crown with strawberries.

Bottom: melon filled with Waldorf salad, orange fillets, walnut and Maraschino cherry—the skewer is garnished with cherry tomatoes— the whole decoration stands on top of a slice of melon with cut out pieces of tomato.

BULB AND ROOT VEGETABLES

POTATO

Currently, there are about 100 varieties of potatoes whose appearance, flavor, and cooking characteristics can be quite different. There are basically two types of potatoes:

Waxy or boiling potatoes: Because they hold their shape, they are excellent for boiling and therefore cube easily (ideal, for example, for making potato salad). When mashed, these potatoes tend to be thick and lumpy.

Floury or baking potatoes: Excellent for baking, roasting, mashing or "french frying". Although they tend to fall apart when boiled, they are light and fluffy when cooked. This category includes the many varieties of Russet (often called Idaho) potatoes.

Some potatoes have characteristics of both types. They hold together when boiled and are moister than baking potatoes. These include the Yukon Gold and Red Pontiac.

New potatoes are small and immature versions of any variety. The variety most often sold as new is the red potato.

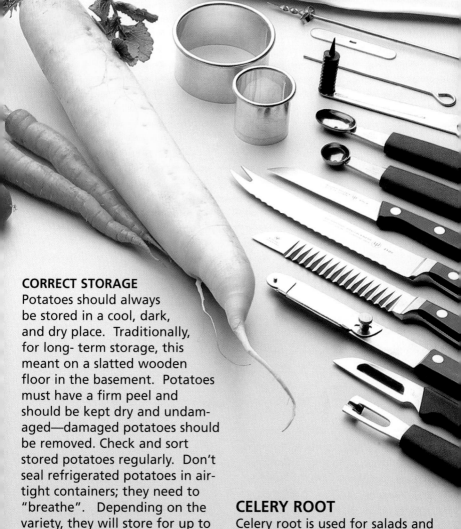

CORRECT STORAGE

Potatoes should always be stored in a cool, dark, and dry place. Traditionally, for long- term storage, this meant on a slatted wooden floor in the basement. Potatoes must have a firm peel and should be kept dry and undamaged—damaged potatoes should be removed. Check and sort stored potatoes regularly. Don't seal refrigerated potatoes in airtight containers; they need to "breathe". Depending on the variety, they will store for up to 60 days before sprouting.

Note: Potatoes bought in a plastic bag should be removed from the bag immediately as this type of packaging is not good for potatoes.

CELERY ROOT

Celery root is used for salads and soups in Europe much more than in North America. Still, it's available almost year round with peak availability from October until April. Fresh roots are firm without any dark areas. If the root sounds hollow when tapped and feels relatively light it's a good bet that it's old and spongy. Brush the celery root under running water before using it and remove long roots and greens. Cut celery root quickly discolors. Adding lemon juice to the water the root is cooked in will prevent discoloration. A whole celery root will last up to one week in the vegetable bin of the refrigerator.

CARROT

Carrots were first cultivated 1,300 years ago in Afghanistan. Today, fresh carrots are available all year, but they're at their best and cheapest in the fall. They are often sold in bunches—including leaves. Carrots stay fresh longer if the leaves are not cut off until shortly before use. Carrots should be stored in a cool and dry place.

CLEANING CARROTS

Young carrots only need to be cleaned with a stiff brush. Older carrots should be peeled with a vegetable peeler.

RADISHES

Radishes are native to China but can grow almost anywhere. Different types of radishes varying in shape, size and taste are offered all year long. The red radish is a dwarf variety most familiar in America. Spring radishes are not as spicy the rest of the year. When buying radishes, make sure they are firm and not spongy or cracked.

TOOLS

Use a pastry bag for mashed potatoes; spiral, and olive shaped cutters, and melon ballers for carrots and celery root. Knifes are used for making decorative cuts.

GARNISHES WITH WHOLE ROOTS AND BULBS

CARROT

Wash and peel a small carrot. Leave about 1⅝" (4 cm) of the leaves. Scrape off any black spots with the tip of a knife and clean the bottom of the leaves.

RADISHES

Thoroughly wash radishes and cut off the root. Remove the outer leaves and keep only the prettiest inner leaves.

Note: The area where the leaves grow out of the radish often contains sand. Remove this sand with the tip of a knife.

LARGE RADISHES

Clean a small specimen of the large radish variety and only leave the prettiest leaves. Wash the radish and evenly peel it using a vegetable peeler. Cover the radish with cold water to prevent wilting.

RADISH BLOSSOMS

Rose: Score the radish skin to make 5 large leaves all the way around, cutting 5 smaller leaves in-between the large ones. Cut out the root in a circular pattern.

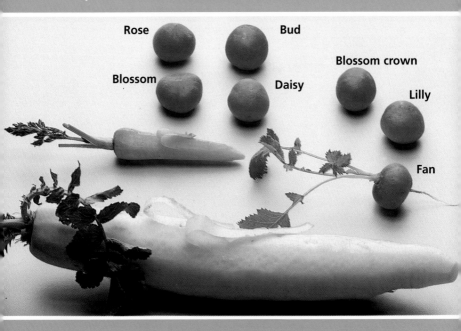

Rose · Bud · Blossom crown · Blossom · Daisy · Lilly · Fan

Blossom: Make incisions into the radish all the way around about ⅛" (3 mm) apart.

Bud: Cut the radish four times lengthwise and six times crosswise through the middle.

Daisy: Score the radish 12 times all the way around, almost all the way down to the stem. Carefully peel the "Daisy leaves" from the flesh of the radish using the tip of a pointed knife. Leave the bottom ends intact.

Blossom crown: Using a pointed knife, pierce the radish all the way to the center in a zigzag pattern. The radish halves come apart easily.

Lilly: Using a channel knife, cut 8 grooves from top to bottom of the radish.

Fan: From the top, make six straight incisions into the radish. Insert a slice of radish in each gap.

Note: Cover cut radishes with cold water—better yet, ice water—to help the "blossoms" unfold completely.

Large radish, small radishes and carrots with leaves; below left: radish rose

Blossom crown

Bud

Blossom

Daisy

Fan

RADISH FLOWER

Slice a small radish and arrange the slices to form a circular blossom. Place a slice of carrot in the middle. Use cucumber peel or steamed onion leaves as the stem and leaves.

Radish flower and lilly

37

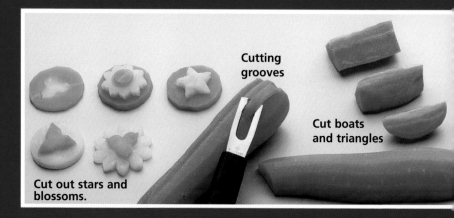

Cutting grooves

Cut boats and triangles

Cut out stars and blossoms.

CUT OUT SHAPES

BALLS

Wash and peel a carrot or celery root. Push an olive shaped cutter or melon baller into the vegetable and using even pressure turn the tool around its axis. Cook the cut out balls in salted water making sure they are still somewhat firm.

STARS AND BLOSSOMS

Slice a cooked carrot or celery root and cut out different shapes (stars, half moons, rosettes, hearts). Arrange the shapes.

GROOVED SHAPES

Select pretty carrots and cook them. Cut grooves down the entire length of each carrot and slice them. Leave the slices whole or cut them in half and arrange them.

CUT SHAPES

Wash and peel a big carrot or celery root. Because celery discolors over time sprinkle it with lemon juice or vinegar.

TRIANGLES

Cook a washed and peeled carrot and cut it in half lengthwise. Cut each carrot half into triangles by holding the knife at an angle to the right and to the left. Arrange the carrot triangles behind one another as a garnish for edges of plates and platters.

LITTLE BOATS

Cut a carrot into $1\frac{5}{8}$ to $1\frac{3}{4}$" (4 to 4.5 cm) long cylinders. Cut the cylinders into quarters lengthwise.

ELLIPSE

Cut the carrot or celery into 1⅝ to 1¾" (4 to 4.5 cm) cylinders or blocks with a diameter of about 1³⁄₁₆" (3 cm). Then, make eight even cuts from top to bottom. First, make half moon shaped cuts on the front and backsides of the block, then on the left and right. Make the next four half moon shaped cuts on the four remaining corners of the block

Cut ellipse

Olive and ball shaped decorations

Balls and cut out shapes

Boats arranged with ball

Cut out, grooved, and cut shapes arranged in rows

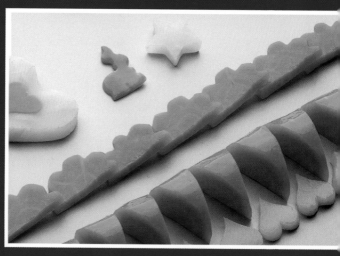

Cut out shapes

Heart shaped cut out

Cut out stars and flowers arranged individually

FRUIT VEGETABLES

TOMATO

Tomatoes, ranging in size from the small Cherry tomato to the giant Beefsteak tomato, are available all year. They are generally red in color but can also be green, pink, yellow and orange. Furthermore, tomatoes are available whole, cut or as paste in cans. There is a vast array of flavors available but none can match the flavor of a tomato ripened on the vine with plenty of sun. These tomatoes are more aromatic than greenhouse tomatoes.

Note: Tomatoes need warm temperatures during their growth and harvest periods as well as in the kitchen. Therefore, it's not preferable to store tomatoes for a long period in the refrigerator.

PEPPERS

There are sweet and hot peppers in various sizes and colors. Sweet peppers are very good raw, but they are also suited for cooking. Hot peppers or chilies are almost exclusively used as a spice. Peppers and chilies are available

all year. They are also available in cans.

EGGPLANT
Eggplant, a member of the potato family, is available year round. It's grown throughout the United States, Europe and Asia. Eggplant comes in different shapes and sizes and its colors range from dark purple to white. Raw eggplant does not taste good. Only through cooking, frying or barbequing does it reveal its nutty flavor and aroma.

AVOCADO
Avocados are harvested when they are still hard and arrive this way in stores. Their full aroma does not unfold until they are fully ripened. The flesh of a ripe avocado has a smooth consistency and a mild, creamy flavor. Therefore, avocados should be kept at room temperature for a few days (about two to eight) before they are used to allow them to fully ripen. If avocados are wrapped in newspaper and stored in a warm place the ripening process only takes two to three days. Ripe avocados keep for a few days in the veg-

etable bin of the refrigerator. An avocado is ripe if it gives slightly when touched. This rule does not apply to the "Hass" variety whose peel is particularly hard.

AVOCADOS IN THE KITCHEN

Avocados are very versatile. They are the perfect ingredient for sweet and hearty salads and may be used in spicy sauces and sweet creams. Avocados also taste good "straight up" with a little salt, pepper and lemon juice. Avocados should not be cut until just before consumption. Sprinkle them with lemon juice immediately after cutting to avoid discoloration.

Note: If avocados are cooked or baked they taste bitter.

TOOLS

Fruit vegetables are peeled and cut with various sizes of knifes. Differently shaped cutters are used to cut decorative shapes of peppers.

GARNISHES WITH CHERRY TOMATO

Cherry or cocktail tomatoes are blanched in the same manner as regular sized tomatoes. Cherry tomatoes may be used to garnish a dish or platter with their skin on or off.

CHERRY TOMATO WITH QUAIL EGG

Cut a cherry tomato in half and carve out the inside. Fill the tomato with half of a hard-boiled quail egg or half of an olive.

BLANCHING TOMATOES

If the tomato is firm cut out the stem in a circular pattern. Make

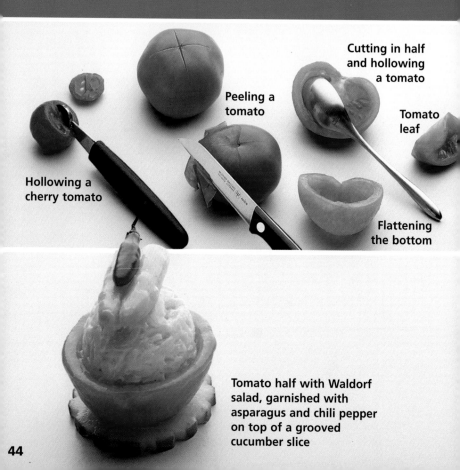

Cutting in half and hollowing a tomato

Peeling a tomato

Tomato leaf

Hollowing a cherry tomato

Flattening the bottom

Tomato half with Waldorf salad, garnished with asparagus and chili pepper on top of a grooved cucumber slice

a superficial, cross-shaped cut on top of the tomato. Place the tomato in boiling water for about 12 to 14 seconds until the skin becomes loose. Immediately place the tomato in cold water. You can now peel off the skin easily.

Note: Peeled tomatoes may be used in the same way as unpeeled tomatoes.

TOMATO HALF FOR STUFFING
Cut a peeled tomato in half lengthwise—from the blossom to the stem. Using a teaspoon or melon baller, scrape out the inside. Flatten the bottom side of the tomato, so that it stands better. Depending on the use of this garnish, place the tomato on top of a slice of cucumber.

TOMATO LEAF
Cut an unpeeled tomato in about six to eight wedges. Remove the seeds from the wedges. Fill and arrange these tomato "leaves" as desired.

TOMATO ROSE
Select a dark red tomato and cut a long piece of peel about ⅝ to ¾" (1.5 to 2 cm) wide by cutting in the shape of a spiral. Roll the strip into a rose blossom by first rolling it tightly and then more loosely—use as a garnish.

Tomato rose

Tomato cut into six wedges, garnished with radish crown and quail egg

Tomato rose on grooved
cucumber slice

Tomato half
filled with silver
onions, cucumber
balls, carrot balls
and strips of
green onion on
top of a grooved
cucumber slice

Cherry tomato
filled with cream
cheese and capers
on top of a
radish crown

Cherry tomato
with quail egg

Tomato rose on a bed
of cress and a slice of lemon

46

SQUASH AND CUCUMBERS

SQUASH

The many different varieties of squash include the large orange pumpkin, butternut squash, acorn squash and spaghetti squash. They are differentiated by size, shape and color. What they all have in common is that the flavor of their flesh is relatively neutral. The flesh of a ripe pumpkin should be bright yellowish-orange, firm, crisp, and juicy—not soft or stringy. A ripe pumpkin should make a sound when tapped. If stored in a cool and dry place, pumpkins may last until winter. To use a pumpkin for cooking, cut the squash from stem to blossom into segments using a big, sharp knife. Scrape out the seeds and stringy inner part with a spoon. Peel the segments before using the flesh. If you want to leave the rind of the pumpkin intact use a sharp spoon to scrape out the flesh.

ZUCCHINI

A zucchini is a cucumber-like, six-sided vegetable harvested before it has fully ripened and the peel is still soft. Zucchinis at this stage have a light to dark green peel, are about 6" (15 cm) long and weigh between 4.5 and 10.5 oz (about 125 to 300 grams). Their flesh is light green and crisp and the seeds in the center are firmly embedded in the flesh. Avoid large zucchinis. Their peel is often yellowish, their flesh spongy and their flavor bland.

Also, do not buy zucchinis that look wilted and shriveled. Fresh zucchinis may be stored for up to eight days in the vegetable bin of the refrigerator.

Note: Zucchinis are never peeled. Without the peel the flesh would disintegrate during steaming, frying or baking. Before cooking remove only the stem and—if present—any brown spots.

CUCUMBER

The cucumber is an old, cultivated plant whose origin is probably in India. The different varieties extend from the small, ridged pickling cucumber all the way to the long, smooth English cucumber. Cucumbers are available all year—however, the selection is most abundant during the summer. The quality of a cucumber does not depend on its size but rather on the firmness of its flesh. A high-quality cucumber has very firm flesh.

For garnishes, you can use fresh English cucumbers as well as pickles.

TOOLS

The olive cutter and melon baller are used for cucumber and zucchini decorations. A channel knife and a corrugated knife are used to create cucumber garnishes. A large knife is used for cutting up squash and cucumbers.

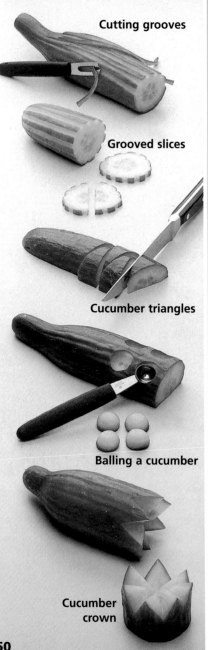

Cutting grooves

Grooved slices

Cucumber triangles

Balling a cucumber

Cucumber crown

DECORATIONS MADE WITH ENGLISH CUCUMBERS

CUCUMBER SLICE
Slice a grooved cucumber and arrange the slices behind one another.

HALVED CUCUMBER SLICES
Cut grooved cucumber slices in half and arrange behind one another on the edge of a platter. The cuts will form a line.

CUCUMBER TRIANGLES
Peel an English cucumber, cut it in half lengthwise, and cut it into triangles. Arrange them behind or next to one another or in a circle.

CUT OUT CUCUMBER
Using an olive shaped cutter or a melon baller, ball a peeled or unpeeled cucumber. Arrange the balls in a circle or as a cluster of grapes. Shape the cucumber peel into "grape leaves". Use olive shaped cucumber bites to fill cucumber boats or hollowed tomatoes.

CUCUMBER CROWN
Cut an unpeeled English cucumber into several 3 to 4" (8 to 10 cm) pieces. Cut the pieces in half by making a zigzag cut all the way around and lightly turning the two halves to separate them.

Cluster of cucumber "grapes"

Grooved slices with shapes cut out of tomatoes

Cucumber in the shape of a flower with a slice of egg and stuffed olive

Cucumber crown with cut mushroom cap

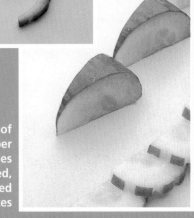

Rows of cucumber triangles and halved, grooved cucumber slices

51

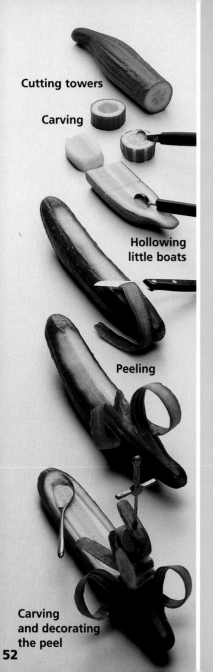

Cutting towers

Carving

Hollowing little boats

Peeling

Carving and decorating the peel

CUCUMBERS FOR STUFFING

CUCUMBER TOWER
Cut the cucumber crosswise into about 1⅝" (4 cm) high towers. Carve out the seeds with a melon baller.

CUCUMER BOAT
Cut a cucumber in half lengthwise and cut 2 to 2⅜" (5 to 6 cm) long pieces. Gently carve out the seeds with a teaspoon or melon baller. Flatten the bottom side of the cucumber half so that it will stand.

WHOLE CUCUMBER
Wash but do not peel a good-looking, medium sized English cucumber. Using a knife or vegetable peeler, cut a thick slice of peel from end to end, but do not cut it off.

Flatten the bottom of the prepared cucumber so that it will stand. From a second cucumber, cut a thick, grooved slice that will be used for the decorative skewer. Tie the peel into a bow; pierce the decorative skewer through the bow and through the vertically wrapped cucumber slice. Attach this roll to the stem end of the cucumber. With a teaspoon, gently carve out the seeds through the entire length of the cucumber and stuff with a colorful salad.

Cucumber tower stuffed with olive-shaped celery and carrot salad

Grooved cucumber tower with cherry tomato and quartered quail egg

Cucumber flower with a slice of egg and stuffed olive

Top: Cucumber boat with a slice of mushroom, cauliflower, broccoli, tomato leaves, and half a quail egg.

Middle: Grooved cucumber tower with mushroom salad.

Bottom: Cucumber stuffed with colorful vegetable salad

MUSHROOMS

MUSHROOMS

Mushrooms are found in brown and white varieties. All varieties taste best when prepared fresh. They may be stored in the vegetable bin of the refrigerator for 3 to 4 days and should not be stored in plastic bags.

WHAT SHOULD YOU KEEP IN MIND WHEN BUYING MUSHROOMS?

At the store, you have the choice between "ready-to-use" and "unprepared" mushrooms.

Ready-to-use mushrooms have closed caps and cut stems. These mushrooms only need to be washed under running water and dried on a kitchen towel. When dry, the stems may be shortened further. Unprepared mushrooms are generally fresher and more aromatic because they have not gone through the cutting process. They, too, need to be washed under running water and well dried. When dry, shorten the stems.

TOOLS
Use a knife and a channel knife to make decorative cuts in mushroom caps.

GARNISHED MUSHROOMS
For garnishes, use medium sized, white mushrooms whose gills are still closed. Thoroughly wash the mushrooms and sprinkle with lemon juice to ensure that they retain their light color longer. If the mushrooms are older with dark spots and a spongy, dry texture cut off the stems until the flesh appears bright and elastic again.

SLICE OF MUSHROOM
Slice washed mushrooms and arrange them behind one another.

GROOVED MUSHROOM CAP
Using a channel knife cut six to eight grooves in the mushroom cap starting from the top center. Sprinkle with lemon juice.

CUT MUSHROOM CAP
Hold the blade of a sharp knife at an angle between thumb and index finger. Make sickle shaped incisions starting from the top center of the cap. Sprinkle with lemon juice.

Grooved mushroom cap filled with a sweet chestnut, a prune, silver onions, and pistachios

Cut mushroom cap; slice of mushroom with carrot and cucumber balls

STUFFED MUSHROOM CAP

To make this garnish, use mushroom caps that are equal in size. Thoroughly wash the mushrooms and cut off the stems. If desired, use the melon baller to hollow the cap a little more and fill.

Variation: Press the stuffing into the mushroom cap and coat it with flour. Sauté the caps in butter and season them with salt and pepper. You can also season the mushroom cap with salt and pepper, coat it with flour, egg, and bread crumbs and deep-fry it.

Cutting grooves

Cutting

Mushroom prepared for stuffing

Mushroom slices with cut out tomato and green pepper shapes

Filled mushroom cap with vegetable balls on top of a cut out slice of green pepper

Grooved mushroom cap on top of cut out cucumber star

Mushroom cap filled with tomato salad

57

BUTTER GARNISHES

BUTTER

Butter is a naturally occurring milk product consisting of skimmed off cream. Butter is made from either fresh or sour cream. Sometimes, salt is added to preserve the butter longer.

TOOLS

Different tools are used to make butter decorations. The multi-purpose butter-garnishing tool combines several tools in one. It is used to make butterballs, corrugated slices or curls. Grooved boards are used to shape butterballs. Butter stamps consist of two parts: a tube and a handle. The handle contains a carved out image. With a butter stamp, simple pieces of butter are embellished with charming designs. Use various cutters to cut pretty shapes from about 3/16" (1/2 cm) thick slices of butter.

CUT BUTTER GARNISHES

Dip the middle part of the multi-purpose butter garnishing tool into boiling water and cut off a slice of butter. The slices will be corrugated on both sides.

CUT OUT BUTTER GARNISHES

Slice the butter and cut out shapes using appropriately sized cutters. Place the shapes in ice water.

Cut out butter

Decorative pieces of butter with a tomato rose

59

Butterballs

Butterballs covered with paprika and herbs

Butter stamp

Butter curls

Butter rose

BUTTER GARNISHES
BUTTERBALLS
Dip the butter-garnishing tool into boiling water, press down on a piece of butter that is not too hard and evenly turn the tool. Place the butterballs in a bowl of ice water. For various decorations, shape butterballs between two grooved boards or coat them with paprika and finely chopped herbs.

CLUSTER OF BUTTER BALLS
You will need about 30 to 40 butterballs to make a cluster. For the stem and leaves, slice the butter using a knife that has been dipped into boiling water. Use a stencil to cut out the desired shapes and arrange them on a plate. Use the back of the knife to imprint veins on the leaves. Arrange the smooth or grooved butter balls in the shape of a grape cluster.

BUTTER STAMPS
Butter that is left over after cutting out shapes can either be used to butter bread or it can be pressed into the butter stamp. Before using it, immerse the butter stamp in cold water for a few minutes. Press the soft butter into the stamp and use the handle to push out a stamped piece of butter.

BUTTER CURLS

Butter curls are made with the curler end of the butter-garnishing tool. To make curls, quickly pull the curler over the butter from one end to the other. Place the curls in ice water.

BUTTER ROSE

Stir room temperature butter to a creamy consistency and then fill a pastry bag with a flat tip with the butter. Stick the blunt end of a 3⅞" (10 cm) sewing needle into a cork and the pointed end into a firm, halved apple. Cover the top of the cork with aluminum foil. Squirt the butter on the cork while carefully turning it, making a small bud. Now make small, inner petals of about 1³⁄₁₆ to 1⅝" (3 to 4 cm) width: squirt the butter in a wave-like manner, moving the tip upward. The outer petals should be a little wider and longer. To make a larger and more open rose blossom, carefully blow on the top of the blossom. When finished, let the blossom set in the refrigerator keeping it on the cork and apple.

Butter roses

Butter curls

Cut pieces of butter with a radish rose

Portioned butter from the butter stamp

Butter balls with paprika and herbs

"Grape cluster" of butterballs

INDEX